THE OFFICIAL
ANNUAL 2019

**Written by Rob
& Barbara Mason
Designed by Tony Carr**

A Grange Publication

© 2018. Published by Grange Communications Ltd.,
Edinburgh, under licence from Sunderland Association
Football Club. Printed in the EU.

Photographs © Getty Images /
Ian Horrocks / Sunderland AFC /
Barbara Mason

ISBN: 978-1-912595-64-8

£8.99

CONTENTS

PLAYER PROFILES

1

JON McLAUGHLIN

Position: Goalkeeper
Date of birth: 9 September 1987
Birthplace: Edinburgh
Last club: Hearts
Previous clubs: Harrogate RA, Harrogate Town, Bradford City, Burton Albion
Clubs on loan to: None
International: Scotland
Did you know? Jon came on as a sub for Bradford in the League Cup final in 2013 and also played in the same season's Play-off final. A double promotion winner with Burton, Jon was in the League One Team of the Year in 2015-16 and made his international debut in 2018.

2

ADAM MATTHEWS

Position: Defender
Date of birth: 13 January 1992
Birthplace: Swansea
Last club: Celtic
Previous clubs: Cardiff City
Clubs on loan to: Bristol City
International: Wales
Did you know?
When he made his debut Adam became the 1,000th player to play a competitive game for Sunderland.

BRYAN OVIEDO

3

Position: Defender / Midfielder
Date of birth: 18 February 1990
Birthplace: Ciudad Quesada, Costa Rica
Last club: Everton
Previous clubs: Saprissa, Copenhagen
Clubs on loan to: Nordsjaelland
International: Costa Rica
Did you know?
Bryan played at the World Cup last summer and once scored the winner for Everton at Manchester United.

GLENN LOOVENS

4

Position: Defender
Date of birth: 22 September 1983
Birthplace: Doetinchem, Netherlands
Last club: Sheffield Wednesday
Previous clubs: Feyenoord, Cardiff City, Celtic, Zaragoza
Clubs on loan to: Excelsior, De Graafschap, Cardiff City
International: Netherlands
Did you know?
At his first club Feyenoord, Glenn was a teammate of former Sunderland goalkeeper Edwin Zoetebier.

ALIM ÖZTÜRK

5

Position: Centre-back
Date of birth: 17 November 1992
Birthplace: Alkmaar, Netherlands
Last club: Boluspor (Turkey)
Previous clubs: SC Cambuur, Trabzonspor, Hearts
Clubs on loan to: 1461 Trabzon
International: Turkey Under 21
Did you know?
Öztürk takes free kicks and has a good shot from long range. He once scored from almost 40 yards in an Edinburgh derby for Hearts against Hibs.

LEE CATTERMOLE

6

Position: Midfielder
Date of birth: 21 March 1988
Birthplace: Stockton
Last club: Wigan Athletic
Previous clubs: Middlesbrough
Clubs on loan to: None
International: England Under 21
Did you know?
Before making his name with Middlesbrough, as a very young player Lee played for the academy at Sunderland. He was the North-East Writers' Association Player of the Year in 2014.

7

CHRIS MAGUIRE

Position: Forward
Date of birth: 16 January 1989
Birthplace: Belshill, Scotland
Last club: Bury
Previous clubs: Aberdeen, Derby Co., Sheffield Wednesday, Rotherham United, Oxford United
Clubs on loan to: Kilmarnock, Portsmouth, Coventry City, Oxford United
International: Scotland
Did you know? Joining Oxford after a loan spell with them, Chris won promotion to League One with the club as well as twice playing for them in the Football League Trophy final.

DYLAN McGEOUCH

8

Position: Midfield
Date of birth: 15 January 1993
Birthplace: Glasgow
Last club: Hibs
Previous clubs: Celtic
Clubs on loan to: Coventry City, Hibs
International: Scotland
Did you know?
Dylan was with both Celtic and Rangers as a youth player. In his second game for Celtic he scored the club's goal of the season after running 70 yards with the ball.

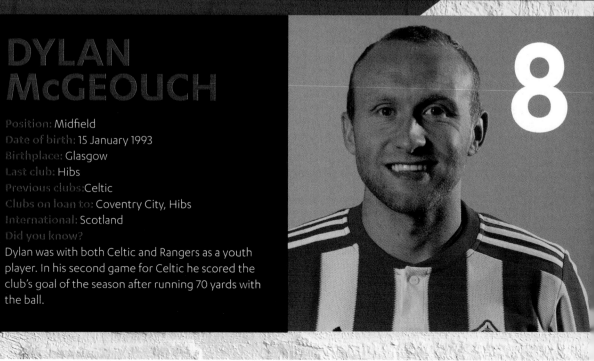

CHARLIE WYKE

9

Position: Forward
Date of birth: 6 December 1992
Birthplace: Middlesbrough
Last club: Bradford City
Previous clubs: Middlesbrough, Carlisle United
Clubs on loan to: Kettering Town, Hartlepool United, AFC Wimbledon
International: None
Did you know?
Charlie's 16 goals for Bradford last season included a hat-trick against Bristol Rovers.

10

GEORGE HONEYMAN

Position: Midfielder
Date of birth: 8 September 1994
Birthplace: Prudhoe
Last club: None
Previous clubs: None
Clubs on loan to: Gateshead
International: None
Did you know?
When George went on loan to Gateshead he played for Sunderland's 1992 FA Cup final manager Malcolm Crosby.

LYNDEN GOOCH

11

Position: Forward
Date of birth: 24 December 1995
Birthplace: Santa Cruz, California
Last club: Santa Cruz Breakers (in youth football)
Previous clubs: Santa Cruz Breakers (in youth football)
Clubs on loan to: Gateshead, Doncaster Rovers
International: USA
Did you know? Although born in California and a full USA international, Lynden has English and Irish parents and first came to Sunderland when he was just 10 years old. He represented the Republic of Ireland at Under 18 level. One of his brothers is a professional surfer.

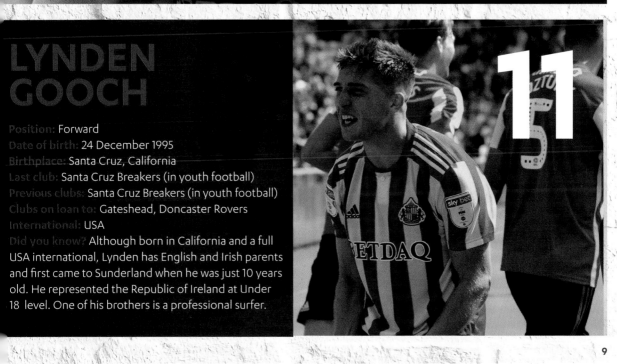

12

TOM
FLANAGAN

Position: Defender
Date of birth: 21 October 1991
Birthplace: Hammersmith, London
Last club: Burton Albion
Previous clubs: MK Dons
Clubs on loan to: Kettering Town, Gillingham,
Barnet, Stevenage, Plymouth Aygyle
International: Northern Ireland
Did you know? Tom made his international debut for
Northern Ireland against New Zealand in June 2017.

13

LUKE
O'NIEN

Position: Midfielder
Date of birth: 21 November 1994
Birthplace: Hemel Hempstead
Last club: Wycombe Wanderers
Previous clubs:Watford
Clubs on loan to: Wealdstone United
International: None
Did you know?
Luke's great uncle Lim Kim San was a famous
politician in Singapore.

14

DUNCAN
WATMORE

Position: Forward   Date of birth: 8 March 1994
Birthplace: Manchester   Last club: Altrincham
Previous clubs: Manchester United (as a young player)
Clubs on loan to: Clitheroe, Curzon Ashton, Hibernian
International: England Under 21
Did you know? 2015 was a brilliant year for Duncan. He
was the U21 Premier League Player of the Season, he
was named 'The Revelation of the Tournament' and also
included in the Team of the Tournament for England
Under 20s in the Toulon Tournament in France. In the
same year he earned a First Class Honours Degree in
Economics and Business Management.

15

JACK
BALDWIN

Position: Defender or midfielder
Date of birth: 30 June 1993
Birthplace: Barking
Last club: Peterborough United
Previous clubs: Faversham Town, Hartlepool United
Clubs on loan to: None
International: None
Did you know?
Jack played exactly 100 league games for his old club
Peterborough, where he was captain.

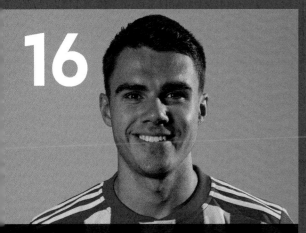

16
REECE JAMES

Position: Defender   **Date of birth:** 7 November 1993
Birthplace: Bacup, Lancashire   **Last club:** Wigan Athletic
Previous clubs: Manchester United plus spells with Rossendale United, Blackburn Rovers and Preston North End as a youth player.
Clubs on loan to: Carlisle United, Rotherham United, Huddersfield Town.
International: None
Did you know? In July 2014 Reece scored twice for Manchester United as they beat LA Galaxy in a friendly. It was his first appearance for the Red Devils. His brother Matty plays for Leicester.

17
JEROME SINCLAIR

Position: Forward
Date of birth: 20 September 1996
Birthplace: Birmingham
Last club: He is on loan from Watford.
Previous clubs: West Bromwich Albion, Liverpool
Clubs on loan to: Wigan Athletic, Birmingham City
International: England Under 17
Did you know?
He became Liverpool's youngest ever player when he debuted six days after his 16th birthday in 2012 at WBA, where he had been a youth player.

18
DONALD LOVE

Position: Defender
Date of birth: 2 December 1994
Birthplace: Rochdale
Last club: Manchester United
Previous clubs: Northwich Town (Youth football)
Clubs on loan to: Wigan Athletic
International: Scotland Under 21
Did you know? Donald played his first game for Manchester United against Sunderland in February 2016, at the Stadium of Light.

19
AIDEN McGEADY

Position: Winger   **Date of birth:** 4 April 1986
Birthplace: Rutherglen, Scotland
Last club: Everton
Previous clubs: Celtic, Spartak Moscow
Clubs on loan to: Sheffield Wednesday, Preston NE
International: Republic of Ireland
Did you know? Aiden's dad John McGeady played for Sheffield United while Aidan has won over 90 caps for the Republic of Ireland after playing for Scotland in an under 13 tournament.

20

JOSH MAJA

Position: Forward
Date of birth: 27 December 1998
Birthplace: Lewisham, London
Last club: Fulham (Junior levels)
Previous clubs: Crystal Palace, Manchester City (Junior levels at both clubs)
Clubs on loan to: None
International: None
Did you know? When he was still 18, Josh scored the winner on his league debut against Fulham, for whom he had played at junior levels when living in London.

21

ETHAN ROBSON

Position: Midfielder
Date of birth: 25 October 1996
Birthplace: Houghton-le-Spring
Last club: None
Previous clubs: None
Clubs on loan to: None
International: None
Did you know? Ethan has worked his way through to the first team having started at the club as an eight-year old. He went to the same school as Jordan Pickford: St. Roberts of Newminster in Washington.

25

ROBBIN RUITER

Position: Goalkeeper
Date of birth: 25 March 1987
Birthplace: Amsterdam
Last club: FC Utrecht
Previous clubs: FC Volendam and as a youth player RKAV Volendam
Clubs on loan to: None
International: None
Did you know?
Robbin experienced Europa League football with FC Utrecht.

27

MAX POWER

Position: Midfielder
Date of birth: 27 July 1993
Birthplace: Birkenhead
Last club: He is on loan from Wigan Athletic
Previous clubs: Tranmere Rovers
Clubs on loan to: Colwyn Bay
International: None
Did you know? Max scored in a penalty shoot-out during his debut for Tranmere against Port Vale in 2011. He has played in at least 45 games in each of the last four seasons and won League One with Wigan last year.

ELLIOT EMBLETON

Position: Midfielder
Date of birth: 2 April 1999
Birthplace: Durham
Last club: Middlesbrough at Under 11 level before returning to Sunderland where he had started.
Previous clubs: None
Clubs on loan to: None
International: England Under 20
Did you know?
The teenager made his first team debut against Wolves just before Christmas in 2017, having first been named on the bench a year earlier at Manchester United. He scored a shoot-out penalty against Ivory Coast to help England Under 20s win the Toulon Tournament in 2017.

29

32

MAX STRYJEK

Position: Goalkeeper
Date of birth: 18 July 1996
Birthplace: Warsaw, Poland
Last club: Polonia Warsaw
Previous clubs: None
Clubs on loan to: Accrington Stanley, Boston United
International: Poland Under 19
Did you know?
Max was called up for Poland's Under 21 squad in 2017.

DENVER HUME

Position: Defender
Date of birth: 11 September 1998
Birthplace: Newbiggin-by-the-Sea
Last club: Ponteland
Previous clubs: Cramlington Juniors
Clubs on loan to: None
International: None
Did you know?
Denver is a skilful player who made his first team debut against Wolves in May 2018.

33

JAKE HACKETT

34

Position: Midfielder
Date of birth: 10 January 2000
Birthplace: Durham
Last club: None
Previous clubs: None
Clubs on loan to: None
International: Selected for England Under 16 training squads.
Did you know?
Jake has been at the club since he was eight, first appearing at Under 18 level in February 2015

35

LUKE MOLYNEUX

Position: Winger
Date of birth: 29 March 1998
Birthplace: Bishop Auckland
Last club: Newton Aycliffe
Previous clubs: None
Clubs on loan to: None
International: None
Did you know?
Sunderland supporter Luke made his debut in the final game of last season in the win over Wolves.

ANDREW NELSON

36

Position: Forward
Date of birth: 16 September 1997
Birthplace: Newton Aycliffe
Last club: None
Previous clubs: None
Clubs on loan to: Hartlepool United, Harrogate Town, Falkirk
International: None
Did you know?
Hard working Andrew was brought up as a Sunderland supporter and last season scored in three of his last five games on loan to Falkirk.

37

BALI
MUMBA

Position: Midfielder
Date of birth: 8 October 2001
Birthplace: DR Congo
Last club: None

Previous clubs: None
Clubs on loan to: None
International: England Under 17
Did you know? When Bali came on as a substitute for his debut on the last day of the season he came on for John O'Shea who gave Bali the captain's armband, making him the youngest captain in the club's history! Bali also became Sunderland's fourth youngest player ever. He has been coming to the SAFC Academy since he was eight and attended Harton Academy.

BRANDON
TAYLOR

40

Position: Defender
Date of birth: 10 May 1999
Birthplace: Gateshead
Last club: Lambton Lions
Previous clubs: None
Clubs on loan to: None
International: None
Did you know?
Brandon grew up supporting Sunderland and has been at the club since he was 11, after which he attended Lord Lawson School.

EARN YOUR STRIPES

Sunderland are known around the world for their famous red and white stripes but red and white were not Sunderland's first colours. When the club first started they wore blue; in fact, their first ground was known as The Blue House Field. It was in 1884 that Sunderland first wore red and white but it was not until 1887 that they wore red and white *stripes*. The first red and white strips were half red and half white. If you think of a Blackburn Rovers kit, it looks a little like that, although of course in red and white, not blue and white!

When they first wore red and white stripes, Sunderland wore white shorts but these quickly changed to black. They remained black from 1888 until 1961. From then on they were again white until December 1972 when they turned black once more. That was the idea of new manager Bob Stokoe, who wanted Sunderland to play in their traditional

strip. Stokoe had the magic touch as just over five months later he managed Sunderland to victory at Wembley, where his team beat Leeds United in the FA Cup final.

In 1981 Sunderland came up with a very different kit which featured red shorts. It went with a mainly white shirt that had very thin red stripes. This lasted two seasons until the black shorts were restored and the shirt went back to normal, apart from having white sleeves. Later there was a version of the kit with red sleeves, with the striped sleeves returning in 1988.

In 2017-18 there was a break with tradition as the famous red and white stripes were made much thinner than norma,l while the back of the shirt lost its stripes altogether and became all red. In 2018 -1 Sunderland again wore red shorts.

Southampton, Stoke City, Sheffield United, Lincoln City and Cheltenham all traditionally wear red and white stripes. So of course, do Sunderland, who have won more major trophies in their history than all of these clubs put together.

Over the years Sunderland's socks have almost always been basically black or red, sometimes with red tops if they were black and white tops if they were red. For approximately the first 50 years of the club, the socks were almost always black but for almost all of the next fifty years they were red until in 1986, they changed to white for a couple of seasons before going red again.

When the Stadium of Light opened in 1997, the socks became black for the first time in almost half a century and they remained black for over a decade before a period where they regularly changed between black and red.

In 2018-19 the red and white stripes became wider again but the back of the top had no stripes at all. The all-red back had a white number. At the beginning of the season it was thought that red shorts would be worn with the home kit but on the first day of the season black shorts were worn in the home win over Charlton Athletic. For the away kit in 2018-19, Sunderland introduced an all-black kit with a red trim.

Which kit is your favourite? Why do you like it? Do your friends prefer different kits? Ask them.

Whichever strip you wear though just make sure it is a Sunderland strip. That's your team, that's where your heart is and when Sunderland win promotion – whenever that is – you will know that you proudly supported your local team when they needed you most.

SPOT THE DIFFERENCE

CAN YOU SPOT THE EIGHT DIFFERENCES IN THE ACTION SHOTS BELOW?

(ANSWERS CAN BE FOUND ON PAGE 61)

2018-19 SQUAD NUMBERS

1 Jon McLaughlin
2 Adam Matthews
3 Bryan Oviedo
4 Glenn Loovens
5 Alim Öztürk
6 Lee Cattermole
7 Chris Maguire
8 Dylan McGeouch
9 Charlie Wyke
10 George Honeyman
11 Lynden Gooch
12 Tom Flanagan
13 Luke O'Nien
14 Duncan Watmore
15 Jack Baldwin
16 Reece James
17 Jerome Sinclair
18 Donald Love
19 Aiden McGeady
20 Josh Maja
21 Ethan Robson
25 Robbin Ruitter
27 Max Power
29 Elliot Embleton
32 Max Stryjek
33 Denver Hume
34 Jake Hackett
35 Luke Molyneux
36 Andrew Nelson
37 Bali Mumba
40 Brandon Taylor

SAMSON'S SUMS

Use Sunderland's squad numbers to work out the sums Samson has set you. Writedown your answers and check them on page 61.

1) George Honeyman + Lynden Gooch

2) Glenn Loovens + Charlie Wyke

3) Chris Maguire + Dylan McGeouch

4) Reece James - Tom Flanagan

5) Max Stryjek - Alim Öztűrk

6) Jack Baldwin - Glenn Loovens

7) Dylan McGeouch + Reece James − Donald Love

8) Jack Baldwin x Tom Flanagan

9) Josh Maja ÷ Alim Ozturk

10) Robbin Ruiter x Adam Matthews x George Honeyman

SQUAD NUMBERS

Traditionally players wore numbers 1 to 11 and way back in the early days of football, players did not have numbers at all. Sunderland first wore squad numbers in the 1993-94 season. The facts here come from the seasons when Sunderland have worn squad numbers. Sunderland have worn squad numbers in every season from 2007-08 and in eight different seasons before then.

18-19 WEARER: Jon McLaughlin
FIRST PLAYER TO SCORE IN THIS NUMBER:
Mart Poom v Derby, 2003

PLAYERS TO WEAR THIS NUMBER INCLUDE:
Tony Coton, **Thomas Sorensen** & Craig Gordon

18-19 WEARER: Adam Matthews
FIRST PLAYER TO SCORE IN THIS NUMBER:
Chris Makin v Spurs, 2000

PLAYERS TO WEAR THIS NUMBER INCLUDE:
Dariusz Kubicki, Stephen Wright & **Phil Bardsley**

18-19 WEARER: Bryan Oviedo
FIRST PLAYER TO SCORE IN THIS NUMBER:
Richard Ord v WBA 1993

PLAYERS TO WEAR THIS NUMBER INCLUDE:
Martin Scott, **Asamoah Gyan** & Patrick van Aanholt

18-19 WEARER: Glenn Loovens
FIRST PLAYER TO SCORE IN THIS NUMBER:
Kevin Ball v Wimbledon 1999

PLAYERS TO WEAR THIS NUMBER INCLUDE:
Gary Bennett, Claudio Reyna & Teemu Tainio

18-19 WEARER: Alim Ozturk
FIRST PLAYER TO SCORE IN THIS NUMBER:
Derek Ferguson v Carlisle 1994

PLAYERS TO WEAR THIS NUMBER INCLUDE:
Steve Bould, **Nyron Nosworthy** & Wes Brown

18-19 WEARER: Lee Cattermole
FIRST PLAYER TO SCORE IN THIS NUMBER:
Kevin Ball v Port Vale 1995

PLAYERS TO WEAR THIS NUMBER INCLUDE:
Paul Butler, Paul McShane & Lee Cattermole

18-19 WEARER: Chris Maguire
FIRST PLAYER TO SCORE IN THIS NUMBER:
Gary Owers v Notts County, 1994

PLAYERS TO WEAR THIS NUMBER INCLUDE:
Nicky Summerbee, **Carlos Edwards** & Seb Larsson

18-19 WEARER: Dylan McGeouch
FIRST PLAYER TO SCORE IN THIS NUMBER: Don Goodman v Middlesbrough, 1993

PLAYERS TO WEAR THIS NUMBER INCLUDE:
Dean Whitehead, **Steed Malbranque** & Craig Gardner

18-19 WEARER: Charlie Wyke
FIRST PLAYER TO SCORE IN THIS NUMBER: Gordon Armstrong v Oxford Utd, 1994

PLAYERS TO WEAR THIS NUMBER INCLUDE:
Niall Quinn, Djibril Cisse & Fabio Borini

18-19 WEARER: George Honeyman
FIRST PLAYER TO SCORE IN THIS NUMBER:
Phil Gray v Aston Villa, 1993

PLAYERS TO WEAR THIS NUMBER INCLUDE:
Kevin Phillips, Kieran Richardson & Jordan Henderson

18-19 WEARER: Lynden Gooch
FIRST PLAYER TO SCORE IN THIS NUMBER:
Craig Russell v Millwall, 1993

PLAYERS TO WEAR THIS NUMBER INCLUDE:
Allan Johnston, Kevin Kilbane & Darren Bent

18-19 WEARER: Tom Flanagan
FIRST PLAYER TO SCORE IN THIS NUMBER:
Danny Dichio v Walsall 1999

PLAYERS TO WEAR THIS NUMBER INCLUDE:
Joachim Bjorklund, Liam Miller and **Adam Matthews**

18-19 WEARER: Luke O'Nien
FIRST PLAYER TO SCORE IN THIS NUMBER: Callum McManaman v Middlesbrough, 2018

PLAYERS TO WEAR THIS NUMBER INCLUDE:
Tony Norman, Darren Ward & **Jordan Pickford**

14

18-19 WEARER: Duncan Watmore

FIRST PLAYER TO SCORE IN THIS NUMBER: Michael Proctor v Wimbledon, 2003

PLAYERS TO WEAR THIS NUMBER INCLUDE: Darren Holloway, **Danny Higginbotham** & Paulo Da Silva

15

18-19 WEARER: Jack Baldwin

FIRST PLAYER TO SCORE IN THIS NUMBER: Alex Rae v Watford, 1996

PLAYERS TO WEAR THIS NUMBER INCLUDE: Carsten Fredgaard, **Danny Collins** & David Vaughan

16

18-19 WEARER: Reece James

FIRST PLAYER TO SCORE IN THIS NUMBER: Alex Rae v Bradford City, 1999

PLAYERS TO WEAR THIS NUMBER INCLUDE: David Kelly, Jason McAteer & **John O'Shea**

17

18-19 WEARER: Jerome Sinclair

FIRST PLAYER TO SCORE IN THIS NUMBER: Niall Quinn v Nottingham Forest, 1996

PLAYERS TO WEAR THIS NUMBER INCLUDE: Jody Craddock, Kenwyne Jones & Danny Welbeck

18

18-19 WEARER: Donald Love

FIRST PLAYER TO SCORE IN THIS NUMBER: Lee Howey v Middlesbrough, 1994

PLAYERS TO WEAR THIS NUMBER INCLUDE: Martin Smith, Darren Williams & **Grant Leadbitter**

19

18-19 WEARER: Aiden McGeady

FIRST PLAYER TO SCORE IN THIS NUMBER: Andy Melville v Millwall, 1994

PLAYERS TO WEAR THIS NUMBER INCLUDE: **Kevin Kyle**, Lorik Cana & Titus Bramble

20

18-19 WEARER: Josh Maja

FIRST PLAYER TO SCORE IN THIS NUMBER: Stefan Schwarz v Sheffield Wednesday 1999

PLAYERS TO WEAR THIS NUMBER INCLUDE: Andy Reid, Keiren Westwood & Ola Toivonen

21

18-19 WEARER: Ethan Robson

FIRST PLAYER TO SCORE IN THIS NUMBER: Gavin McCann v Leicester City, 1999

PLAYERS TO WEAR THIS NUMBER INCLUDE: Paul Thirlwell, Modibo Diakite & **Yann M'Vila**

22

18-19 WEARER: N/A

FIRST PLAYER TO SCORE IN THIS NUMBER: Martin Smith v Luton Town, 1993

PLAYERS TO WEAR THIS NUMBER INCLUDE: Simon Mignolet, **Sebastian Coates** & Wahbi Khazri

23

18-19 WEARER: N/A

FIRST PLAYER TO SCORE IN THIS NUMBER: Darren Williams v Leicester City, 1997

PLAYERS TO WEAR THIS NUMBER INCLUDE: Nicolas Medina, Roy O'Donovan & Lamine Kone

24

18-19 WEARER: N/A

FIRST PLAYER TO SCORE IN THIS NUMBER: Sean Thornton v Chelsea, 2003

PLAYERS TO WEAR THIS NUMBER INCLUDE: George McCartney, Trevor Carson & Carlos Cuellar

25

18-19 WEARER: Robbin Ruiter

FIRST PLAYER TO SCORE IN THIS NUMBER: Chris Waddle v Everton, 1997

PLAYERS TO WEAR THIS NUMBER INCLUDE: Sotirios Kyrgiakos & Louis Saha

26

18-19 WEARER: N/A

FIRST PLAYER TO SCORE IN THIS NUMBER: Allan Johnston v Everton, 1997

PLAYERS TO WEAR THIS NUMBER INCLUDE: Michael Proctor, Thomas Myhre & Anton Ferdinand

27

18-19 WEARER: Max Power

FIRST PLAYER TO SCORE IN THIS NUMBER: Michael Reddy v Luton Town, 2000

PLAYERS TO WEAR THIS NUMBER INCLUDE: Thomas Butler, Ahmed Elmohamady & **Jan Kirchhoff**

28

18-19 WEARER: N/A

FIRST PLAYER TO SCORE IN THIS NUMBER: John Oster, v Luton Town, 2000

PLAYERS TO WEAR THIS NUMBER INCLUDE: Dan Smith, Stephane Sessegnon & **Jermain Defoe**

29

18-19 WEARER: Elliott Embleton

FIRST PLAYER TO SCORE IN THIS NUMBER: Eric Roy v Walsall, 1999

PLAYERS TO WEAR THIS NUMBER INCLUDE: Tom Peeters, Peter Hartley & Valentin Roberge

30

18-19 WEARER: N/A

FIRST PLAYER TO SCORE IN THIS NUMBER: No player had scored wearing this number up to the start of 2018-19

PLAYERS TO WEAR THIS NUMBER INCLUDE: **Lionel Perez**, Jurgen Macho & Will Buckley

31

18-19 WEARER: N/A

FIRST PLAYER TO SCORE IN THIS NUMBER: Michael Reddy v Middlesbrough, 1999

PLAYERS TO WEAR THIS NUMBER INCLUDE: Milton Nunez, Christian Bassila & **David Connolly**

32

18-19 WEARER: Max Stryjek

FIRST PLAYER TO SCORE IN THIS NUMBER: Stan Varga v West Ham United, 2001

PLAYERS TO WEAR THIS NUMBER INCLUDE: Justin Hoyte, **Marton Fulop** & Max Stryjek

33

18-19 WEARER: Denver Hume

FIRST PLAYER TO SCORE IN THIS NUMBER: Julio Arca v West Ham United, 2000

PLAYERS TO WEAR THIS NUMBER INCLUDE: Jan Eriksson, Ross Wallace & Lee Cattermole

34

18-19 WEARER: Jake Hackett

FIRST PLAYER TO SCORE IN THIS NUMBER: Dwight Yorke v Stoke City, 2006

PLAYERS TO WEAR THIS NUMBER INCLUDE: George McCartney, Kevin Kyle & Tommy Robson

35

18-19 WEARER: Luke Molyneux

FIRST PLAYER TO SCORE IN THIS NUMBER: No player had scored wearing this number up to the start of 2018-19

PLAYERS TO WEAR THIS NUMBER INCLUDE: Charalampos Mavrias, **Josh Maja** & Jake Clarke-Salter

36

18-19 WEARER: Andrew Nelson

FIRST PLAYER TO SCORE IN THIS NUMBER: Emerson Thome v Coventry City, 2000

PLAYERS TO WEAR THIS NUMBER INCLUDE: Richie Ryan, Nathan Luscombe & Marc Wilson

37

18-19 WEARER: Bali Mumba

FIRST PLAYER TO SCORE IN THIS NUMBER: No player had scored wearing this number up to the start of 2018-19

PLAYERS TO WEAR THIS NUMBER INCLUDE: Jonjo Dickman, Robbie Weir & **Rees Greenwood**

38

18-19 WEARER: N/A

FIRST PLAYER TO SCORE IN THIS NUMBER: Michael Bridges v Stoke City, 2004

PLAYERS TO WEAR THIS NUMBER INCLUDE: Ben Clark, Craig Lynch & Mikael Mandron

39

18-19 WEARER: N/A

FIRST PLAYER TO SCORE IN THIS NUMBER: George Honeyman v Bury, 2017

PLAYERS TO WEAR THIS NUMBER INCLUDE: Jon Kennedy, Martyn Waghorn & Lee Cattermole

40

18-19 WEARER: Brandon Taylor

FIRST PLAYER TO SCORE IN THIS NUMBER: No player had scored wearing this number up to the start of 2018-19

PLAYERS TO WEAR THIS NUMBER INCLUDE: Michael Ingham, **Mart Poom** & Louis Laing

41

18-19 WEARER: N/A

FIRST PLAYER TO SCORE IN THIS NUMBER: Duncan Watmore v Norwich City, 2015

PLAYERS TO WEAR THIS NUMBER INCLUDE: Patrick Collins, Michael Liddle & David Meyler & Phil Bardsley.

42

18-19 WEARER: N/A

FIRST PLAYER TO SCORE IN THIS NUMBER: No player had scored wearing this number up to the start of 2018-19

PLAYERS TO WEAR THIS NUMBER INCLUDE: Jordan Henderson, John Egan & Liam Agnew

43

18-19 WEARER: N/A

FIRST PLAYER TO SCORE IN THIS NUMBER: No player had scored wearing this number up to the start of 2018-19

PLAYERS TO WEAR THIS NUMBER INCLUDE: Conor Hourihane

44

18-19 WEARER: N/A

FIRST PLAYER TO SCORE IN THIS NUMBER: Anthony Stokes v Northampton Town, 2008

PLAYERS TO WEAR THIS NUMBER INCLUDE: Jonny Evans & Adnan Januzaj

45

18-19 WEARER: N/A

FIRST PLAYER TO SCORE IN THIS NUMBER: Rade Prica v Birmingham City, 2008

PLAYERS TO WEAR THIS NUMBER INCLUDE: Jordan Cook & Josh Robson

46

18-19 WEARER: N/A

FIRST PLAYER TO SCORE IN THIS NUMBER: No player had scored wearing this number up to the start of 2018-19

PLAYERS TO WEAR THIS NUMBER INCLUDE: Nick Colgan & **Lynden Gooch**

48

18-19 WEARER: N/A

FIRST PLAYER TO SCORE IN THIS NUMBER: No player had scored wearing this number up to the start of 2018-19

PLAYERS TO WEAR THIS NUMBER INCLUDE: Joel Dixon & **Josh Robson**

52

18-19 WEARER: N/A

FIRST PLAYER TO SCORE IN THIS NUMBER: Nicklas Bendtner v WBA, 2011

PLAYERS TO WEAR THIS NUMBER INCLUDE: Only Nicklas Bendter had worn number 52 up to the start of 2018-19.

53

18-19 WEARER: N/A

FIRST PLAYER TO SCORE IN THIS NUMBER: Ovie Ejaria v Wolves, 2018

PLAYERS TO WEAR THIS NUMBER INCLUDE: Only Ovie Ejaria had worn number 53 up to the start of 2018-19

FAMOUS FANS

Every Sunderland supporter is a famous fan because the Red and White army are famous in football. Did you know these well-known people all support Sunderland?

MELANIE HILL

LAUREN LAVERNE

SIR TIM RICE

Melanie Hill went to Monkwearmouth Academy which is next to SAFC's Academy of Light. She is an actor who you might have seen in Coronation Street, Emmerdale, The Bill, Waterloo Road, Hebburn or maybe Bread.

A former pupil at St. Anthony's School, Lauren Laverne was a singer and guitarist in a rock band called Kenickie. Now she is a DJ on BBC 6 Music and presents TV programmes including Glastonbury Festival.

Working with various partners, Tim Rice wrote 'Joseph and the Amazing Technicolour Dreamcoat', 'Jesus Christ Superstar' and 'Evita'. He also worked on the music for 'The Lion King' and he has a star on the Hollywood Walk of Fame. He is a trustee of the Foundation of Light.

GEORGE CLARKE

KATE ADIE OBE DL

TV presenter George Clarke attended Oxclose Community Academy in Washington, supports Sunderland and is a trustee of the Foundation of Light. On TV he appears on lots of programmes including, 'George Clarke's Amazing Places'.

Kate Adie is a very famous TV news reporter who covered many war zones, showing great bravery. She is a big supporter of Sunderland and is a trustee of the Foundation.

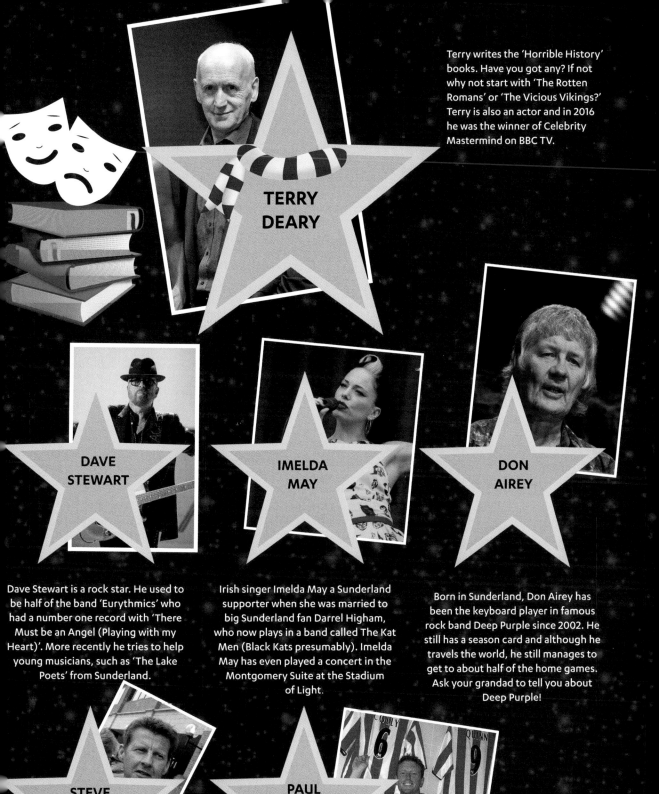

TERRY DEARY

Terry writes the 'Horrible History' books. Have you got any? If not why not start with 'The Rotten Romans' or 'The Vicious Vikings?' Terry is also an actor and in 2016 he was the winner of Celebrity Mastermind on BBC TV.

DAVE STEWART

IMELDA MAY

DON AIREY

Dave Stewart is a rock star. He used to be half of the band 'Eurythmics' who had a number one record with 'There Must be an Angel (Playing with my Heart)'. More recently he tries to help young musicians, such as 'The Lake Poets' from Sunderland.

Irish singer Imelda May a Sunderland supporter when she was married to big Sunderland fan Darrel Higham, who now plays in a band called The Kat Men (Black Kats presumably). Imelda May has even played a concert in the Montgomery Suite at the Stadium of Light.

Born in Sunderland, Don Airey has been the keyboard player in famous rock band Deep Purple since 2002. He still has a season card and although he travels the world, he still manages to get to about half of the home games. Ask your grandad to tell you about Deep Purple!

STEVE CRAM CBE

PAUL COLLINGWOOD MBE

As an athlete Steve Cram set world records in the 1500 and 2000 metres as well as the mile. He also won a Gold medal at the World Championships and a silver at the Olympics. He was BBC Sports Personality of the Year in 1983. Nowadays he presents sport on BBC TV and is also a trustee of the Foundation of Light.

Paul Collingwood is a famous cricketer who played for England and once scored 207 against Australia. He is a massive Sunderland fan and a trustee of the Foundation.

PUZZLE TIME

CAN YOU MATCH UP THE TEAM TO THE NICKNAME?

Here are seven sides Sunderland face this season and a list of nicknames.
Can you put the right nickname next to the right team?

BLACKPOOL	POMPEY
BRISTOL ROVERS	POSH
LUTON TOWN	THE CHAIRBOYS
PETERBOROUGH UNITED	THE HATTERS
PORTSMOUTH	THE PIRATES
SOUTHEND UNITED	THE SHRIMPERS
WYCOMBE WANDERERS	THE TANGERINES

This Sunderland player's name has become all jumbled up. Can you put the letters into the right order to work out who it is?

HRCSI   GREMUAI

COLOUR CODED

These League One teams play in red, blue, yellow and green but can you match the right colour to the right club?

PLYMOUTH ARGYLE

CHARLTON ATHLETIC

GILLINGHAM

OXFORD UNITED

GUESS WHO...

Can you guess who the 3 Sunderland players are in this jumbled up picture?

A

B

C

BADGE OF HONOUR

Can you pair the badge to the following clubs?

FC WIMBLEDON, ACCRINGTON STANLEY, BARNSLEY, BRADFORD CITY, BURTON ALBION, COVENTRY CITY

Puzzle Time answers can be found on page 61.

RECORD BREAKERS

BOBBY GURNEY

KEVIN PHILLIPS

EUROPEAN GOLDEN SHOE WINNER

In 1998-99 Kevin Phillips won the European Golden Shoe as the top scorer in all of Europe's top leagues. Superkev became the first Englishman to win the award after scoring 30 times in a season in the Premier League.

TOP GOAL-SCORER

Bobby Gurney scored an incredible 228 goals for Sunderland between 1926 and 1938. 31 of his goals came in 1935-36 as he helped Sunderland win the league (what is now known as the Premier League). A year later, he scored Sunderland's first ever goal at Wembley as Sunderland won the FA Cup.

CHARLIE BUCHAN

TOP LEAGUE GOAL-SCORER

Charlie Buchan scored even more league goals than Bobby Gurney. Buchan helped Sunderland win the league and reach the FA Cup final in the same season of 1912-13. In total Buchan scored 222 goals, which is six less than Gurney, but his total of league goals was 209, four more than Gurney.

DAVID HALLIDAY

TOP GOAL-SCORER IN A SEASON

David Halliday scored a fantastic 43 goals for Sunderland in the 1928-29 season. The scorer of Sunderland's second highest total in a season scored 42 times and the third best was 39. Halliday was also the player who scored those second and third highest totals!

JIMMY MONTGOMERY

RECORD APPEARANCE MAKER

Goalkeeper Jim Montgomery played an astonishing 627 games for Sunderland between 1961 and 1976. Left back Len Ashurst played the second highest number of times. His 458 appearances make him Sunderland's record outfield appearance maker.

JIMMY HAMILTON

YOUNGEST GOAL-SCORER

Jimmy Hamilton was even younger than Bali Mumba and Joel Asoro when they set their records when he became Sunderland's youngest ever goal-scorer. The Scottish forward was only 16 years and 103 days old when he came off the bench to score the winner in a 4-3 win over Preston in 1971 – before he dashed out of the ground to get the bus home to the place he was staying.

JOEL ASORO

YOUNGEST PREMIER LEAGUE PLAYER

Joel Asoro became the youngest player to play in the Premier League for Sunderland when he played against Middlesbrough at the Stadium of Light in August 2016, when he was 17 years and 117 days old.

BALI MUMBA

YOUNGEST PLAYER AT THE STADIUM OF LIGHT

Bali Mumba became the youngest player to play at the Stadium of Light for Sunderland when he came on as a substitute in the last game of last season against Wolves, when he was only 16 years and 210 days old. What's more, Bali became Sunderland's youngest captain as he was handed the skipper's armband by John O'Shea who was being substituted.

DEREK FORSTER

YOUNGEST PLAYER

Derek Forster was only 15 years and 185 days old when he made his debut for Sunderland in August 1964. Forster was a goalkeeper and the match against Leicester was at the same level the Premier League is now. Leicester's goalkeeper was England international Gordon Banks!

THOMAS URWIN

OLDEST PLAYER

Thomas Urwin made his final appearance for Sunderland when he was 39 years and 76 days old. The game was against Preston in 1935.

BRYAN 'POP' ROBSON

OLDEST SCORER

Bryan 'Pop' Robson was 38 years and 183 days old when he set the record as Sunderland's oldest scorer when he scored at Leicester in May 1984.

ACADEMY OF LIGHT

THE ACADEMY OF LIGHT IS SUNDERLAND AFC'S TRAINING BASE.

IT IS ONE OF THE BIGGEST AND BEST TRAINING GROUNDS IN THE COUNTRY.

YOUNG PLAYERS ARE DEVELOPED HERE WITH THE AMBITION THAT THEY WILL DO WELL ENOUGH TO PROGRESS INTO THE FIRST TEAM.

LAST SEASON NINE HOME PRODUCED PLAYERS PLAYED FOR THE FIRST TEAM.

JORDAN HENDERSON AND JORDAN PICKFORD FROM ENGLAND'S 2018 WORLD CUP SQUAD WERE DEVELOPED AT THE ACADEMY OF LIGHT.

THE ACADEMY OF LIGHT WAS OPENED IN 2003 BY SVEN-GORAN ERIKSSON, WHO AT THE TIME WAS MANAGER OF ENGLAND.

INTERNATIONAL TEAMS HAVE TRAINED AT THE ACADEMY WHEN PLAYING AT THE STADIUM OF LIGHT.

THERE IS A LARGE INDOOR TRAINING BARN WITH A 4G SYNTHETIC PITCH, IDEAL FOR DEVELOPING THE SKILLS OF VERY YOUNG PLAYERS DURING BAD WINTER WEATHER.

THERE IS ALSO AN OUTDOOR ALL-WEATHER PITCH.

THE NUMBER OF OUTDOOR PITCHES MARKED OUT CAN VARY BUT THERE CAN BE UP TO 18 PITCHES AVAILABLE, INCLUDING A SHOW-PITCH THAT COMPETITIVE UNDER-18 & SOMETIMES UNDER-21 MATCHES ARE PLAYED ON.

INSIDE FACILITIES INCLUDE A HYDROTHERAPY POOL, GYM AND OUTSTANDING MEDICAL FACILITIES.

THERE ARE ALSO CHANGING ROOMS, A FIRST TEAM PLAYERS' LOUNGE, AN ACADEMY PLAYERS' GAMES ROOM, OFFICES, CATERING AREAS AND A MEDIA AREA.

THE FOYER OF THE ACADEMY INCLUDES A RANGE OF ITEMS FROM THE CLUB'S HISTORY INCLUDING INTERNATIONAL SHIRTS AND TROPHIES WON BY YOUTH TEAMS.

PROMOTION RACE

CAN YOU HELP SUNDERLAND WIN PROMOTION?

Play this game and see if you can get The Lads back into the Championship at the first attempt.

Just like when you you play football you need to get your kit ready, to play this game you need to get a dice and something to use as a counter for each player.

START YOUR SEASON HERE!

5 Sloppy start, go back five places.

7 Good pass, have another roll of the dice.

11 You win your first game. Go forward three places

15 Surprise new signing on transfer deadline day, have an extra turn

17 Your goalkeeper injured closes transfer window with swap deal. You move whole places after it. It's your last, miss a turn

20 You hit form, have three turns in a row and ignore anything it says on the squares you land on until your last go

23 Your captain is suspended. Roll the dice & go back as many spaces as the dice says.

GAME RULES

- Each player rolls the dice. Whoever gets the highest score goes first.

  If two or more people have the same highest score, those people have another go each until someone wins.

  Once you 'kick-off,' after the first player's turn it is the person on their left who goes second. Continue in that direction until you are back to the person who started.

  Every player has to get a six before they can put their counter on the board, which they do by going straight to square six.

  The winner is the first person to win promotion.

42 You are disappointed to only draw but find all your rivals have lost, have forward one space.

41

40

39 The fans help you. The a crucial three to a forward three if you Move forward if you Move, but only if you spaces, shout 'Ha'way the Lads' three times really loudly.

43

44 Not the time to lose a key game, move back three spaces.

38

37

31 You miss a key last minute penalty, miss a turn.

32

33

34

35 You are boosted with a brand new signing in the January transfer window, move forward four spaces.

36

30

29

...van winner, move forward two places!

...injury time, move forward two places!

45

46 **Last game of the normal season!** If you land here first, you have won the league providing you can get a 2, 3, 4, 5 or 6 with an extra roll of the dice. If you get a 1 you go into the Play-offs so move to square 49. Anyone else reaching square 46 after you now has to get to square 49.

47

48

49 **It's the Play-off final!** Wait for someone else to also reach square 49. Then each roll the dice to find out the score of the final & see who wins. If you both get the same score, roll again until you have a winner.

33

THE STADIUM OF LIGHT

SUNDERLAND'S STADIUM IS ONE OF THE VERY BEST IN THE COUNTRY. IT WAS THE BIGGEST AND BEST STADIUM BUILT IN ENGLAND IN THE SECOND HALF OF THE TWENTIETH CENTURY.

WHEN IT OPENED IN 1997 IT HELD 42,000 PEOPLE.

WHEN IT WAS BUILT THE STADIUM WAS CONSTRUCTED SO THAT IT COULD BE EXTENDED IN THREE STAGES. IF THE SECOND AND THIRD STAGES EVER HAPPEN, WITH THE SOUTH AND EAST STANDS DEVELOPED AS THE NORTH STAND HAS BEEN, THE CAPACITY COULD CLIMB TO AROUND 66,000!

AFTER THREE SEASONS THAT CAPACITY WASN'T BIG ENOUGH. THE NORTH STAND WAS EXTENDED SO THE GROUND COULD ACCOMMODATE JUST UNDER 49,000 PEOPLE.

THE MAN WHO WAS RESPONSIBLE FOR SUNDERLAND HAVING THE STADIUM OF LIGHT AND THE TRAINING BASE, THE ACADEMY OF LIGHT, WAS SIR BOB MURRAY CBE. WITHOUT HIM SUNDERLAND WOULD PROBABLY BE STUCK IN A SMALL FOOTBALL GROUND THAT WOULD BE 120 YEARS OLD. WHILE THE OLD GROUND WAS FULL OF HISTORY IF SUNDERLAND WERE STILL THERE IT WOULD BE LIKE GOING TO A MUSEUM NOT A MATCH. DO YOU KNOW WHAT THE OLD GROUND WAS CALLED? IF YOU DON'T, ASK SOME OLDER MEMBERS OF YOUR FAMILY TO TELL YOU ABOUT IT.

BELGIUM, TURKEY AND AUSTRALIA HAVE ALL PLAYED ENGLAND AT THE STADIUM OF LIGHT. ENGLAND HAVE A 100% RECORD AT THE STADIUM.

KEVIN PHILLIPS, NIALL QUINN, JULIO ARCA, STEFAN SCHWARZ, CLAUDIO REYNA, MICHAEL GRAY, JERMAIN DEFOE, JORDAN HENDERSON AND JORDAN PICKFORD ARE JUST SOME OF THE PLAYERS TO HAVE STARRED FOR SUNDERLAND AT THE STADIUM OF LIGHT.

SAM ALLARDYCE, DICK ADVOCAAT, ROY KEANE, PETER REID, STEVE BRUCE, CHRIS COLEMAN, GUS POYET & PAOLO DI CANIO ARE JUST SOME OF THE MANAGERS TO SIT IN THE SOL HOT-SEAT.

UP AND

Jordan Henderson and Jordan Pickford are the crown jewels of players produced at the Academy of Light. Many other great players have come through the Sunderland Youth system since the Academy opened in 2003, but what about the next generation?

Here we feature some young players hoping to make their names having come through the Academy of Light.

BALI MUMBA

Midfielder Mumba made a name for himself before he even kicked a ball for Sunderland. Coming on for his debut in the final minute of the 2017-18 season, he replaced outgoing captain John O'Shea on the former skipper's final appearance for the club. Recognising that Mumba represented the future, O'Shea handed Bali the captain's armband, making the youngster technically the youngest captain in the club's history – although he was only captain for a minute!

At the age of 16 years and 210 days when he made his bow against Wolves, Bali became the fourth youngest player ever to represent Sunderland. Only Derek Forster, Jimmy Hamilton and Cecil Irwin have been younger than South Shields-raised Bali when they made their debut.

ELLIOT EMBLETON

England Under-20 international midfielder Elliot Embleton went to school in Durham and will be 20 on April 2nd. He is able to use both feet and is an excellent passer of the ball. Having started to come onto the radar during in the 2016-17 season when he scored an excellent goal at Rochdale in the Checkatrade Trophy and was on the bench several times in the Premier League, last season Elliott played in both Championship games against Wolves, as well as appearing in the FA Cup against Middlesbrough.

COMING

LUKE MOLYNEUX

Winger Luke Molyneux made his debut on the last day of the 2017-18 season. Oddly enough, his first game was against Wolverhampton Wanderers, whose home ground is called Molineux! Originally he was due to be on the bench in that game but an injury to Kazenga LuaLua led to Luke being told he was starting. Having been given the chance, Molyneux made the most of it with the sort of exciting display the Bishop Auckland born player will have dreamed of ever since he started coming to the match with his grandad, who is a season card holder at the Stadium of Light.

DENVER HUME

Like Luke Molyneux and Bali Mumba, Denver Hume got his chance on the last day of last season with a debut against Wolves. A naturally gifted player with quick feet and fine balance, left back Hume had been at Sunderland for over half of his life when his debut came along. Denver comes from Newbiggin, near Ashington, a town in Northumberland with a footballing history that includes former Footballer of the Year and Sunderland manager Jimmy Adamson, as well as World Cup winners Bobby and Jackie Charlton and Newcastle legend Jackie Milburn. Full back Cecil Irwin, who played over 300 games for Sunderland, came from nearby Ellington. If Denver can do half as well as him he'll have done brilliantly.

ACADEMY ACES

Sunderland have some of the very best training facilities in the country at the Academy of Light. First team footballers use the academy to do their work when they are not actually playing matches at the Stadium of Light or away from home. The academy is also where Sunderland's coaching staff try to develop players from as young as eight years of age.

Skills are worked on for many years and each season some players are considered good enough to stay on for another season. Eventually young players get to play for the Under 18 team, the Under 23 team and hopefully one day, the first team.

Sometimes players don't do so well at Sunderland but come back to enjoy successful careers elsewhere. Other players start at Sunderland and then are transferred to other clubs and sometimes players stay at Sunderland having come through the youth system.

Here are just a few modern day players who started at the Academy of Light

JORDAN HENDERSON

Liverpool captain, who has also captained England, midfielder Henderson is from East Herrington, went to Farringdon School and played 79 games for Sunderland before being bought by Liverpool for a reported £16m in 2011.

JORDAN PICKFORD

Everton and England goalkeeper, Jordan Pickford starred for Sunderland before being sold for a reported record fee of £30m in 2017. He gained a lot of experience by going on loan, as well as playing for Sunderland's junior sides and has many years at the top level ahead of him.

MARTYN WAGHORN

Martyn Waghorn came through the youth system at the same time as Jordan Henderson. He became the youngest player to appear for Sunderland in the Premier League when he made his debut against Manchester United on Boxing Day in 2007. He became a big hero at Glasgow Rangers and spent last season at Ipswich. He signed for Derby County in August.

CONOR HOURIHANE

Captain of Aston Villa and a Republic of Ireland international, Conor came to Sunderland from his home city of Cork. A talented midfielder, he did not play a league or cup game for Sunderland or his second club Ipswich but used the skills he had developed at the Academy to work his way back to the top by showing his ability with Plymouth and Barnsley before joining Villa.

JOHN EGAN

Captain of Brentford in 2017-18 and now a Republic of Ireland international, Egan was sold to Sheffield United in the summer. Like Hourihane, John did not play for Sunderland but gained experience on loan to Crystal Palace, Sheffield United, Bradford City and Southend United - where he won the goal of the season award - while he was developing at Sunderland. After moving to Gillingham, John was Player of the Year in his first season and was named in the PFA League One Team of the Year in his second year.

GEORGE HONEYMAN

Always a talented player with plenty of skill on the ball, George has developed into a hard working player who really came into his own at Sunderland last season. In what was a difficult year for the team, George, who is from Prudhoe in Northumberland, never gave up and managed to score some important goals along the way. His first five goals were all scored away from home, helping his team to three wins and two draws, but after the last of that run in a 4-1 win at Derby George got his first goals at the Stadium of Light in the next two home games. He is now Sunderland's captain.

LYNDEN GOOCH

An international player for the USA, Lynden has an English father and an Irish mother. It was through his mother that Lynden's first international experience was for the Republic of Ireland at Under-18 level. Although he was born in California he started coming to Sunderland's academy when he was just ten years old. He played in the Premier League for Sunderland and like George Honeyman, last season he showed the sort of fighting spirit the team will need as they fight for promotion. Again like Honeyman, Gooch gained experience as a loan player at Gateshead and also played for Doncaster. Lynden's birthday is on Christmas Eve.

JOEL ASORO

A Sweden Under-21 international who scored twice against Turkey in March 2018, Joel took Martyn Waghorn's record as Sunderland's youngest Premier League player when he made his debut against Middlesbrough in 2016. At the same time he also became the youngest player from Sweden to appear in the Premier League. A very quick forward, Asoro impressed last season when he was a bright spot for the team in a tough season and scored his first goal in a 1-0 win over Hull City at the Stadium of Light in January 2018. Still a teenager until the end of April in 2019, Joel came to Sunderland after being with Bromma and IFK Haninge as a very young player in Stockholm. He was sold to Swansea in the summer.

BEACON OF LIGHT

The brand new Beacon of Light stands next to the Stadium of Light.

It is the base for work done by the Foundation of Light charity which uses the power of football to do good in the community.

Step inside the Beacon and you walk down a street of opportunities. There are zones for sport, education, health & well-being as well as the world of work.

There are facilities for

7

different sports at the Beacon.

The Beacon includes a 12-court sports hall and a seven-a-side 4G pitch on the roof!

Outside there are

6

five-a-side pitches and two multi-use games areas.

FOUNDATION OF LIGHT

THE WORLD AT YOUR FEET

Helping people gain qualifications and skills to help them get work is all part of what the Beacon is for.

In the Education Zone people can learn together whether they are young, old or in between!

The Beacon of Light is the first of its kind in the UK and was opened for everyone in the North East.

The World of Work at the Beacon aims to make people more confident and help them to get a good job.

The Beacon is there to help people to be healthier. This includes helping people to stop smoking and help them with weight issues.

The Beacon will be spectacularly lit up at night. Watch out for it turning red and white!

BAKE OFF WITH

Samson & Delilah Show You How To Make A Football Scarf Cake

You will need:

175g soft butter/ margarine plus 1 teaspoon extra for greasing the tin

175g caster sugar

3 eggs

175g self-raising flour

25g icing sugar

1 tube red writing icing

250g ready to roll red icing

250g ready to roll white icing

2 tablespoons jam

To make it you will also need:

Kitchen scales

mixing bowl

food mixer or wooden spoon

sharp knife

rolling pin

spatula

baking tin approx. 20cm X 30cm

Make sure you have an adult to help.

Switch on the oven at set it at 175°c/350°f/Gas 4

Wash your paws!

1 Carefully weigh all your ingredients and have them ready to use.

2 Grease the tin with a teaspoon of butter/margarine.

3 Put the remaining butter/margarine in the mixing bowl with the caster sugar, flour and eggs and using the mixer or your wooden spoon beat the mixture till it becomes smooth and creamy and there are no lumps left. This will take a few minutes.

SAMSON & DELILAH

4 Scrape all the mixture into the baking tin and smooth the top with your spatula or the back of a spoon and carefully put the cake in the oven.

5 Bake for 25 – 30 minutes until the cake is golden and firm.

6 Take the cake out of the oven and leave to cool completely.

7 When the cake is completely cold cut it in half lengthways and lay each piece side by side to make a long rectangle.

8 Use a knife to spread the jam over the top and sides of the cake.

9 On a clean surface sprinkle a fine layer of icing sugar and spread some on your rolling pin. (This will stop the icing from sticking). Lay the red icing on your surface and roll it out to a rectangle 15cm X 30cm. Cut this widthways into 6 equal strips. Repeat this with the white icing cutting 5 strips the same size as the red ones.

0 Lay red and white strips onto your cake in alternate stripes, starting and ending with red. They should stick to the jam surface.

1 Use the remaining strips to cut into fringes and stick onto both ends of the cake.

12 Finally use your writing icing to pipe S A F C onto the white stripes.

Enjoy sharing your cake with your friends!
Made by Samson & Deliliah (AKA Hairy Berry)

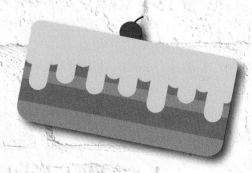

SUNDERLAND SOUVENIRS

On display at the Stadium of Light are many rare and often unusual items from Sunderland's history. You can find medals, trophies, international caps, strips, old tickets and programmes and many more things from Sunderland's rich past.

Most of these items are on display, mainly in the foyer of the stadium and in Quinn's Bar at the ground. Sunderland also have some famous items on display at their training ground, the Academy of Light

SEASON TICKET FROM 1888-89

Have you got a season card this season? Having one has always been the best way of making sure you never miss a home game. Season cards – or season tickets as they used to be known – have been around for a very long time. This one is from 130 years ago! This season ticket for the 1888-89 season was before Sunderland even joined the Football League.

LEAGUE TITLE MEDAL FROM 1893

During the 1890s Sunderland were known as 'The Team of All The Talents' and won the league title for three years out of four. This medal from the 1892-93 season is especially important as it is from the only year in which Sunderland won the title for a second successive season. This medal belonged to a famous player called Jimmy Hannah who was the team's second top scorer that season with 18 goals.

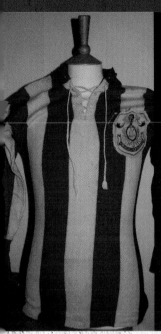

SHIRT WORN IN THE 1913 FA CUP FINAL

Sunderland have played in four FA Cup finals. This one is from Sunderland's first cup final in 1913. Back then the FA Cup was mainly known as the English Cup. It was worn by a famous player called Harry Low. Sunderland lost the cup final 1-0 to Aston Villa – but they were league champions for a fifth time that season.

1937 FA CUP WINNERS MEDAL

The first time Sunderland won the FA Cup was in 1937. They beat Preston North End 3-1 in the final at Wembley. This medal was won by a player called Sandy McNab, who was a Scottish international.

CHARLIE HURLEY'S REPUBLIC OF IRELAND INTERNATIONAL CAP

Charlie Hurley was voted Sunderland's Player of the Century in 1979. Only modern day player Seb Larsson of Sweden has won more international caps while with Sunderland than Hurley, who won 38 of his 40 caps while with Sunderland, including this one against Spain.

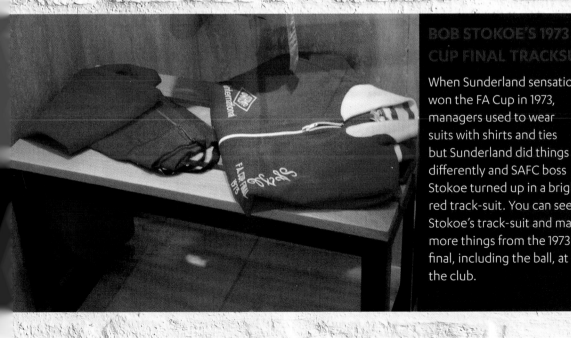

BOB STOKOE'S 1973 FA CUP FINAL TRACKSUIT

When Sunderland sensationally won the FA Cup in 1973, managers used to wear suits with shirts and ties but Sunderland did things differently and SAFC boss Stokoe turned up in a bright red track-suit. You can see Stokoe's track-suit and many more things from the 1973 cup final, including the ball, at the club.

CHRIS
MAGUIRE

7

ALBANIA:
Lorik Cana

ARGENTINA:
Julio Arca

AUSTRALIA:
Willie Fraser

AUSTRIA:
Jurgen Macho

BELGIUM:
Simon Mignolet

BENIN:
Stephane Sessegnon

BRAZIL:
Emerson Thome

COSTA RICA:
Bryan Oviedo

ZIMBABWE:
Benjamin Mwaruwari

GREENLAND (DENMARK)

CZECH REPUBLIC:
Ondrej Celustka

ZAMBIA:
Iain Hesford

WALES:
Andy Melville

USA:
Claudio Reyna

URUGUAY:
Sebastian Coates

TUNISIA:
Wahbi Khazri

CANADA

UNITED STATES OF AMERICA

MEXICO

BRAZIL

PERU

BOLIVIA

PARAGUAY

CHILE

URUGUAY

ARGENTINA

SCOTLAND
Jim Baxter

TRINIDAD & TOBAGO:
Dwight Yorke

SWITZERLAND:
Bernt Haas

SWEDEN:
Seb Larsson

SOUTH KOREA:
Ji Dong-won

SOUTH AFRICA:
Steven Pienaar

SPAIN:
Marcos Alonso

SLOVAKIA:
Stanislav Varga

SENEGAL:
El-Hadji Diouf

ENGLAND:
Dave Watson

EGYPT:
Ahmed
Elmohamady

ESTONIA:
Mart Poom

FINLAND:
Teemu
Tainio

FRANCE:
Lilian
Laslandes

GABON:
Didier
Ndong

GERMANY:
Jan
Kirchhoff

GHANA:
Asamoah
Gyan

DENMARK:
Thomas
Sorensen

GREECE:
Charis
Mavrias

GUADELOUPE:
Pascal
Chimbonda

HONDURAS:
Milton
Nunez

HUNGARY:
Marton
Fulop

INDIA:
Leslie
McDowall

RUSSIA

KAZAKHSTAN

MONGOLIA

CHINA

JAPAN

INDIA

TAIWAN

GUAM

PHILIPPINES

MALAYSIA

INDONESIA

AUSTRALIA

NEW
ZEALAND

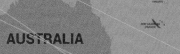

ITALY:
Fabio Borini

ROMANIA:
Costel
Pantilimon

**REPUBLIC
OF IRELAND:**
Charlie
Hurley

POLAND:
Dariusz
Kubicki

PARAGUAY:
Paolo Da
Silva

NORWAY:
Tore Andre
Flo

**NORTHERN
IRELAND:**
Martin
Harvey

NIGERIA:
Reuben
Agboola

NETHERLANDS:
Bolo Zenden

MOROCCO:
Talal El
Karkouri

BLACK CAT ACADEMY

ARE YOU A MEMBER OF THE BRAND NEW BLACK CAT ACADEMY?

Just as at Sunderland there is the first team, the Under 23 team and the Under 18 team (as well as younger age groups) there are three age groups within the Black Cat Academy.
Which one are you in?

0 TO 5 YEARS OLD

6 TO 11 YEARS OLD

12 TO 16 YEARS OLD

WHAT DO YOU GET WHEN YOU JOIN THE BLACK CAT ACADEMY?

A contract from manager Jack Ross

The chance to be a mascot on a matchday (6-12 year olds)

The chance to take part in junior job roles

Members only events

The chance to join a Black Cat Committee fan forum

Your own special age related section on safc.com

Manager Jack Ross knows how important it is to have young supporters. He says, "I remember the excitement of going to my first match as a young supporter and meeting players. It would be fantastic to see as many youngsters as possible getting behind the team and showing their support and hopefully our junior membership scheme will encourage a whole new generation of Sunderland fans."

JOIN UP

Joining the Black Cat Academy costs £20 per member. You can join the Black Cat Academy by calling the ticket office on 0371 911 1973 or for more information, visit www.safc.com/blackcatacademy or email blackcatacademy@safc.com

BE A MASCOT

If you are a member of the 6 to 12 years old section of the Black Cat Academy there is a chance to be a mascot at a game. This costs £150 and for this you get:

* To walk out with the team

* Two tickets for the game

* A full junior kit

* A mini-tour

* Matchday photographs

* A match programme

* The day's team-sheet

Ask an adult to email blackcatacademy@safc.com if you are interested.

Don't worry. You don't have to buy one of these packages to have a chance of being a mascot. One mascot per game is also selected at random from Black Cat Academy members so you might be lucky and find it is you. There is no charge for the lucky member.

THE FIRST WORLD CHAMPIONS

YOU MAY WELL JOIN IN THE CHANT THAT SAYS 'SIX LEAGUE TITLES AND STILL GOING STRONG' BUT DID YOU KNOW SUNDERLAND WERE THE FIRST WORLD CHAMPIONS?

Although Sunderland haven't done well recently, still to this day only Manchester United, Liverpool, Arsenal, Everton and Aston Villa have been champions of England more times than Sunderland.

Right from the very early days of League football Sunderland were a powerhouse. Sunderland were the first club to be champions three times. That was The Team of All The Talents. They were champions in 1892, 1893 and 1895, as well as being runners' up in 1894.

While football is now played around the world, at this time, only three countries were officially playing the game: England, Scotland and Argentina. Although Argentina have been a world power in modern times, back in the 1890s the standard of football there was far short of that in England and Scotland.

Top English and Scottish clubs had played before but when Sunderland met Hearts in 1895 it was the first time the reigning champions of Scotland and England had played each other and so it was the world championship of the club game.

Heart of Midlothian had the advantage of the game being played at their Tynecastle Ground but Sunderland were a superb team and determined to prove they were the best in the game.

Goals from Harry Johnston and all-time great Johnny Campbell put Sunderland two goals ahead but Hearts were a great side themselves and came back to lead 3-2, Robert McClaren scoring twice after Willie Taylor had pulled a goal back.

Another all-time great Sunderland player – Jamie Millar – made it three all before Sunderland once again built up a two goal lead, Robert McNeil scoring twice to make the final score: Hearts 3-5 Sunderland.

Sunderland, 'The Team of All The Talents' were not just champions of England, they were champions of the world.

PROMOTION DREAM

POSITION AT THE END OF EACH MONTH	
AUGUST	1ST
SEPTEMBER	10TH
OCTOBER	1ST
NOVEMBER	1ST
DECEMBER	1ST
JANUARY	1ST
FEBRUARY	1ST
MARCH	2ND
APRIL	1ST
MAY	1ST

PLAYER OF THE YEAR

Eric Gates had not done well in his first two seasons at Sunderland after signing from Ipswich, where he had been a star player when Ipswich were a top team. Once Gates was partnered with new signing Marco Gabbiadini he showed what a class act he was. His quality on the ball was miles better than anyone else in the division and Gabbiadini made the most of playing alongside him.

TOP SCORER

Marco Gabbiadini wasn't even at Sunderland when the first eight league games were played but after signing from manager Denis Smith's old club York the young forward scored 21 goals in 35 games and got another goal in a cup game.

This season Sunderland are in League One. It is only the second time The Lads have ever played at this level. Back in 1987-88, when what is now League One was called Division Three, Sunderland won the league.

VERSUS

THE G-FORCE

When young striker Marco Gabbiadini was signed he soon found he had a great understanding with Eric Gates. Former England international Gates was an old head who had the talent to provide the passes that Gabbiadini liked to run on to and out-pace opposition defences. Between them the 'G-Force' scored 40 league goals as they blew defences away.

THE MANAGER

Former York manager Denis Smith took over at the start of the season and produced an exciting attacking team. As a player Smith had been a centre-half with Stoke City.

BIGGEST WIN

SUNDERLAND 7
SOUTHEND UNITED 0

Former England international Eric Gates scored four goals as Sunderland slaughtered Southend 7-0 in a game which saw debuts for Richard Ord and Mick Heathcote. Paul Atkinson scored a couple of goals with Marco Gabbiadini also on the mark. Sunderland also scored seven in a Sherpa Van Trophy win over Rotherham.

QUIZ TIME

Rate your red and whiteness.
How can you do on our test?

1 When Jack Ross was appointed Sunderland's manager last summer which club did he leave?

a) St. Johnstone
b) St. Mirren
c) Stranraer

2 Who was Sunderland's first signing of the summer?

a) Alim Öztürk
b) Jon McLaughlin
c) Chris Maguire

3 Who was Sunderland's first game of the season against?

a) Luton Town
b) Scunthorpe United
c) Charlton Athletic

4 Which Championship team did Sunderland meet in the first cup tie of the season?

a) Sheffield United
b) Sheffield Wednesday
c) Middlesbrough

5 Which current Premier League team did Sunderland beat 3-0 on the final day of last season?

a) Wolves
b) Fulham
c) Cardiff City

6 Jon McLaughlin is an international with which country?

a) England
b) Northern Ireland
c) Scotland

7 Sunderland won 1-0 away to which team in the final game of 2017?

a) Nottingham Forest
b) Norwich City
c) Burton Albion

8 Former captain John O'Shea moved to which club during the summer?

a) Rotherham United
b) Bristol City
c) Reading

9 Alim Ozturk has played in all of the countries below but which country was he playing in last season?

a) Netherlands
b) Scotland
c) Turkey

10 Which of the following clubs has Chris Maguire NOT played for?

a) Aberdeen
b) Sheffield Wednesday
c) Barnsley

*Find the answers on page 61
and see how you have done.*

YOUR SCORE

10	CHAMPIONS
9	AUTOMATIC PROMOTION
8	PLAY-OFF WINNER
7	PLAY-OFF FINALIST
6	PLAY-OFF SEMI-FINALIST
5	JUST MISSED OUT
4	MID-TABLE
3	READ YOUR ANNUAL A BIT MORE TO CLIMB THE TABLE
2	RELEGATED
1	BOTTOM

SECOND HALF

Sunderland kick off the second half of the season on Boxing Day when Bradford City are the visitors at the Stadium of Light. Boxing Day is a day when big crowds usually come to the match. In fact the first time an attendance of over 40,000 attended the Stadium of Light for a league game was in the first year of the stadium in 1997 – for a match against the same team Sunderland entertain this year – Bradford.

It is important to have had a positive first half of the season but being top at Christmas guarantees nothing. It is where you are at the end of the season that counts, so the second half of the season is where games have an extra importance. This is because as fixtures begin to run out there is less of a chance of being able to win a promotion position if things don't go right as there are fewer and fewer opportunities. The crowd gets louder as supporters understand the stakes get higher. This makes being at the match even more special.

Sunderland have a great chance to start the second half of the season well as the first two games after Christmas are both at home. Three days after Bradford's visit the Stadium of Light welcomes Shrewsbury Town. They are a good team who played at Wembley twice last season but lost both times. As well as reaching the final of the Checkatrade Trophy where they lost to Lincoln City, The Shrews lost the Play-off final to Rotherham United.This was unlucky for Shrewsbury who had finished third in the league, eight points ahead of fourth placed Rotherham.

The first weekend of

2019

sees Sunderland due to play in London at Charlton Athletic. This day is also due to be the third round of the FA Cup. If either Sunderland or Charlton have won through the first two rounds this game will be re-arranged for later in the season.

Sunderland's first away game

of the second half of the season is on New Year's Day and it is a big one: away to Blackpool. Many supporters will be heading to the Seaside resort hoping to get 2019 off to a bright start.

2019 FIXTURES:

JANUARY

BLACKPOOL (A) - TUE 1ST, 3PM

CHARLTON ATHLETIC (A) - SAT 5TH, 3PM

LUTON TOWN (H) - SAT 12TH, 3PM

SCUNTHORPE UNITED (A) - SAT 19TH, 3PM

GILLINGHAM (H) - SAT 26TH, 3PM

FEBRUARY

AFC WIMBLEDON (H) - SAT 2ND, 3PM

OXFORD UNITED (A) - SAT 9TH, 3PM

ACCRINGTON STANLEY (H) - SAT 1ST, 3PM

BRISTOL ROVERS (A) - SAT 23RD, 3PM

MARCH

PLYMOUTH ARGYLE (H) - SAT 2ND, 3PM

WYCOMBE WANDERERS (A) - SAT 9TH, 3PM

BARNSLEY (A) - TUE 12TH, 7.45PM

WALSALL (H) - SAT 16TH, 3PM

FLEETWOOD TOWN (A) - SAT 23RD, 3PM

BURTON ALBION (H) - SAT 30TH, 3PM

The first
home
league game of 2019 is against Luton Town on January 12th. Luton are a club who have in the past played at the top level and even once won the League Cup at Wembley. Last season they were promoted from League Two. The month finishes with a trip to last season's Play-off semi-finalists Scunthorpe and a home match with Gillingham, although if the Lads are still in the FA Cup there could be exciting cup fixtures to fit in.

February
sees four planned games with AFC Wimbledon and Accrington Stanley making their first ever visits to the Stadium of Light and Sunderland travelling to Bristol Rovers. Before that, they head to Oxford United, the clubSunderland chairman Stewart Donald was once part owner of.

March
is normally one of the busiest months of the season. As the end of the campaign draws near games have more and more importance. With six games to fit in and coming at a time when many teams have suspensions and injuries to cope with, this is often a period when the strength of your squad is of extra importance. During March there are first ever visits to Wycombe and Fleetwood as well as a Tuesday night match at Barnsley. Meanwhile at home, Sunderland welcome Plymouth Argyle, Walsall and Burton Albion.

April
begins with an away game at Rochdale and the visit of former FA Cup winners Coventry City. At Easter Sunderland play twice in four days, welcoming Doncaster Rovers on Good Friday before travelling to Peterborough United on Easter Monday. The month ends with the last home game of the season (Unless there is a Play-off match) when Portsmouth visit on April 27th. For many years 'Pompey' were a successful club. They have twice been champions of England and have won the FA Cup three times, most recently in 2008, as well as being finalists in 2010.

The season ends with a trip to Southend United. Their Roots Hall ground is not the smallest in League One but at 12,000, If Sunderland need a result to win promotion or are celebrating a promotion party it simply won't be big enough and tickets for away supporters will be like gold dust. Fingers crossed that whatever happens in the second half of the season Sunderland can win promotion, ideally without having to take part in the play-offs!

APRIL
ROCHDALE (A) - SAT 6TH, 3PM
COVENTRY CITY (H) - SAT 13TH, 3PM
DONCASTER ROVERS (H) - FRI 19TH, 3PM
PETERBOROUGH UNITED (A) - MON 22ND, 3PM
PORTSMOUTH (H) - SAT 27TH, 3PM

MAY
SOUTHEND UNITED (A) - SAT 4TH, 3PM

*FIXTURES ARE SUBJECT TO CHANGE

FOCUS ON FOUR

Every match is important and the same number of points are on offer no matter who you play but some games stand out as particularly vital. Here we focus on four fixtures to look out for.

LUTON TOWN
HOME
SATURDAY JANUARY 12

The start of a new year always brings new hope. Winning the first home game of a new calendar year can help build momentum as the team look to secure a promotion position. Sunderland don't have a home game in 2019 until 12 days into the year (unless there is a third-round FA Cup tie) but when it does arrive the opening match is a good one. Luton Town were runners up in League Two last season when their free-scoring football made them an attractive side to watch. Sunderland have a good record at home to Luton having won 19, drawn seven and lost only three of The Hatters' trips to Wearside.

ACCRINGTON STANLEY
HOME
SATURDAY FEBRUARY 16

While Sunderland are the biggest club in League One, Accrington Stanley are the smallest. To their great credit Accrington won League Two last season through being brilliantly organised and very hard-working. Accrington were formed in 1968. Another team from Accrington had been Founder Members of the Football League in 1887-88. Way back in the 1890s those clubs met eight times. Sunderland won the last six meetings, scoring 25 goals in those half-dozen games. Their visit to Sunderland in mid-February comes at a vital time of the season as teams fight for places in the promotion race. Accrington could come and shock the football world by beating Sunderland at the Stadium of Light and it is up to Sunderland to show respect to Stanley but make sure they are professional and take the three points.

PLYMOUTH ARGYLE
HOME
SATURDAY MARCH 2ND

Plymouth have only ever won twice at Sunderland – but those victories came in their last three visits. Argyle are a well-supported team whose fans will have travelled over 400 miles to come to Sunderland to follow their team. They will be tricky opponents as Sunderland start the vital month of March when 18 points are available as The Lads head for the finishing line of the season hoping to be in the top two and securing an automatic promotion place.

PORTSMOUTH
HOME
SATURDAY APRIL 27

The final home game of the season would be a very important one regardless of who the visitors were but the visit of Portsmouth brings to Sunderland one of the biggest clubs in the division. Pompey will be hoping to win promotion themselves and with Sunderland aiming for a top-two slot this late-season show-down this match could well be a real six-pointer and one where the stakes are really high. After this match Sunderland still have one game to play at Southend, but all being well Portsmouth's visit will be the last home game of the season. If Sunderland have to win promotion through the Play-offs,
then a Play-off semi-final at the Stadium of Light would be the biggest home game of the year, one where the tension would be amazing but that is a tension most supporters would prefer to do without if Sunderland could win automatic promotion and make the stay in League One as short as possible.

QUIZ & PUZZLE ANSWERS

PAGE 18: SPOT THE DIFFERENCE

PAGE 20: SAMSON'S SUMS

21   2) 13   3) 15   4) 4   5) 27

11   7) 6   8) 180   9) 4   10) 500

PAGE 26: PUZZLE TIME

CKNAMES

ACKPOOL = THE TANGERINES

RISTOL ROVERS = THE PIRATES

JTON TOWN = THE HATTERS

ETERBOROUGH UNITED = POSH

ORTSMOUTH = POMPEY

OUTHEND UNITED = THE SHRIMPERS

YCOMBE WANDERERS = THE CHAIRBOYS

his Sunderland player's name has become all jumbled
. Can you put the letters into the right order to work
t who it is?

RCSI   GREMUAI = CHRIS MAGUIRE

OLOUR CODED

ese League One teams play in red, blue, yellow and
een but can you match the right colour to the right
ib?

YMOUTH ARGYLE = GREEN

HARLTON ATHLETIC = RED

LINGHAM = BLUE

KFORD UNITED = YELLOW

GUESS WHO

A) Bali Mumba   B) Donald Love   C) George Honeyman

BADGES

CAN YOU FIT THE BADGE TO THE CLUB?

  COVENTRY CITY

  BARNSLEY

  AFC WIMBLEDON

  BURTON ALBION

  BRADFORD CITY

  ACCRINGTON STANLEY

PAGE 56 QUIZ TIME

1)   B   St. Mirren
2)   A   Ozturk
3)   C   Charlton
4)   B   Sheffield Wednesday
5)   A   Wolves.
6)   C   Scotland
7)   A   Nottingham Forest
8)   C   Reading
9)   C   Turkey
10)   C   Barnsley